SAIL

in a week

Wendy Fitzpatrick

Headway · Hodder&Stoughton

ACKNOWLEDGEMENTS

The author and publishers would like to thank Champion
Photography for the text photographs, Beken of Cowes Ltd for the
cover illustration, and Gecko Ltd for the artwork.

British Library Cataloguing in Publication Data
Fitzpatrick, Wendy
  Sailing in a week.
  1. Sailing
  I. Title
  797.124

ISBN 0 340 52303 4

Colour originator by Sota Graphic Arts Ltd.
Typeset and illustrated by Gecko Ltd, Bicester, Oxon
Printed in Great Britain for Hodder and Stoughton Ltd, Mill Road,
Dunton Green, Sevenoaks by Clays Ltd, St Ives plc

CONTENTS

INTRODUCTION

Sailing is one of those pastimes which can evoke extremes of feeling: exhileration, fear, boredom, confusion, love and loathing . . . and quite possibly all these in one single person during one single outing!

But at the end of the day it has been a lot of fun. Nature's elements have been met and harnessed and a skill has been learned. A skill which just might become addictive. Be warned.

Be warned, too, right from the start, that water and wind can be enemies as well as friends. Both need our utmost respect and understanding.

Oh yes, sailing *is* fun but **there is no short cut to becoming a competent sailor.** This book takes you through the basics in a logical route, such as might be found at a good sailing school. But, for the sake of easy reading, we must assume a "week" of perfect light breezes.

Having mastered all the boat handling skills in these pages, you will be able to call yourself a **competent beginner**. Sorry, but you will need hours and years of practice and experience before you are an expert. And even experts get it wrong sometimes.

Author's Note

I have avoided technical terms as much as possible, introducing them only when necessary to make the text flow more freely. I hope that this will make it possible for you to dip in to later chapters to find the answers to questions which are bound to crop up as you battle through the basics.

I have deliberately glossed over many aspects of advanced sailing technique and seamanship in favour of explaining the basics as thoroughly as possible in the space available. There are many good books on the various branches of the sport when the time comes to extend your technical knowledge.

I have also used the words "he" and "him" to refer to the helmsman and crew to make the text more readable when it refers to both sexes. I hope no-one will find their use offensive.

HOW TO START

You can plough a lonely furrow . . . go off and buy a boat, launch it and learn the hard way. Sometimes it works. Usually it doesn't. Occasionally it proves fatal.

The best possible way is to enrol for a course at a sailing school and learn by laughter. Learning with others is great entertainment. Suddenly you don't feel such a fool when you get it wrong. Everybody is making the self-same mistakes.

You'll pick up the jargon, experience different types of boats — all of them suitable for the novice — and generally have a good time for very little cost.

What to sail

An afternoon spent at a popular launching site is all you need to realise the enormous number of ways in which people go afloat. Even if we discount power craft — this is, after all, a book about sailing — the variety of boats is vast.

So we'll concentrate on the type which best suits the novice. A small dayboat such as the little Mirror dinghy which we have chosen for the illustrations, is excellent provided the sailors themselves are not large adults. Bigger people need bigger boats, within reason, such as the Wayfarer, her smaller sister the Wanderer or the GP Fourteen (GP stands for General Purpose).

The evergreen GP Fourteen, a stable boat for the family or beginner, which nevertheless enjoys keen racing

There is no reason to discount a singlehanded dinghy. Their tendency to capsize more often can itself be regarded as a teaching aid! The 11 ft Topper is ideal for youngsters and small adults. The Laser, preferably with one of its smaller rigs, gives larger folk more leg room.

The 11 ft Topper deserves its success. Tough, light and fun, it is quick to respond and easy to right after the inevitable capsize. No wonder so many sailing schools use them

For the full-size adult seeking a singlehander, the Laser is a good choice – but it is a high performance boat and may need to be 'detuned' by setting one of its smaller sail alternatives in the early days

Children can learn to sail on their own from as young as six, but real enthusiasm comes with a greater attention span from the age of eight or nine. The ideal child's boat is an Optimist. It is small, easily handled and very stable. It also offers serious international racing if a competitive streak develops.

Whatever your choice of boat, don't make that choice alone. Take the unbiased advice of an experienced sailor. And the best place to find one is at a good sailing school or an active sailing club.

With as many as a hundred different small boat designs still represented around the coasts, a club cannot hope to offer fleet racing to all of them. Most clubs allow their fleets to develop within a handicap fleet, giving them a separate race when their numbers and enthusiasm warrant it. This natural selection process usually means up to half a dozen dinghy designs rule the local roost at any one time.

Even if it is not your first choice, there is a lot to be said for buying a design which enjoys fleet racing at your local club. Re-sale will not be a problem and there will be plenty of experts on hand to help you learn the ropes.

The roomy, stable Wayfarer is an ideal boat for the novice and for a family. She will carry four with ease

Where to sail

There are some good reasons to start sailing on inland water. A lake or landscaped gravel pit is potentially safer than the open sea in that it has no means of escape. Without waves, there is greater scope for sailing in strong winds earlier than would be advisable at sea.

However, many of us prefer the challenge and freedom of sea sailing and as long as sense is used, it does provide a stimulating learning environment.

Whatever the venue, the strongest recommendation we can make is to join a sailing club. Visit your nearest ones and see which makes you welcome. As well as offering somewhere to park the boat, rescue boat cover, hot showers and après-sail refreshment, club membership brings the bonus of the companionship and advice of other sailors, even if some of that advice has to be taken with a liberal pinch of salt.

Where to find clubs and schools

Everywhere. All round the coast and on most sizeable lakes there will be a sailing club, some grand, some no more than a wooden hut.

The Royal Yachting Association in Eastleigh, Hampshire, knows of all the sailing clubs in the country, many of which are also teaching establishments. The **RYA** also keeps a register of sailing schools, which offer a high standard of instruction to its national curriculum.

Clothing

Assuming first steps are to be taken in the summer, expensive specialist gear is not essential to begin with. Trousers which are not too tight, sports socks, old trainers with soft, non-slip soles, shirt, sweater, windproof and splashproof anorak and a good buoyancy aid is the right sort of uniform. Later, when the sailing bug has really bitten, a wetsuit is a good investment and may even be available secondhand. They do cost rather a lot new.

Do keep warm. It is always cooler at sea than on the shore. Keep the body warm especially. Shorts are OK on a fine day but trousers give a little protection against bruises. Never go afloat barefoot. A moment's lapse of concentration arising from a stubbed toe can lead to trouble. Never go afloat without a good buoyancy aid. Take advice on this from the man in the shop: make sure it fits snugly, meets European safety specifications and is not too bulky.

But before we go any further, a word about. . .

The weather

Weather to . . or weather not to. . .

The weather must be the sailor's first thought. Never mind whether or not it is raining. There is a good chance of getting wet anyway. We are interested in wind strength and direction.

We are even more interested in whether either will change during the time we plan to be afloat.

Last night's weather summary after the mid-evening news will have given a good indication of the weather pattern around the country. It was almost certainly accurate but of necessity, television forecasting paints with a broad brush, to please all viewers.

But it does show the accurate position of high and low pressure areas and all you need to worry about to begin with is how close together the isobars are. Isobars are lines drawn to link areas with the same pressure. Air moves from an area of high pressure to an area of low pressure, to try to balance things out. Moving air is wind.

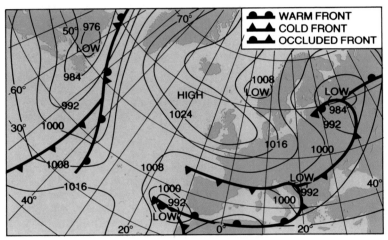

A typical weather chart

When isobars are close together, strong winds can be expected in that area.

When the pressure reading on your barometer drops sharply, very strong winds can be expected.

An up to date forecast for inshore waters is available round the clock by telephone. Directory Enquiries will provide the number for your local Marinecall service.

The more you listen to these forecasts and translate them into your own experiences afloat, the more you will realise that the range of windspeeds in which it is possible to enjoy sailing a small boat is actually quite small.

In windspeeds below about 3 mph, life on a sailing boat can become quite boring, sails slatting like something out of the Ancient Mariner's tale. Winds above about 16 mph are strictly for experts.

Not quite flat calm but not very interesting nevertheless.
Winds of less than about 5mph call for the utmost
concentration. Many sailors just don't bother to go afloat!
These are Contender singlehanders

Often, the windspeed is quoted in knots — that is, nautical miles per hour. One nautical mile is slightly longer than one statute (land) mile. A windspeed of ten knots is equivalent to about eleven and a half miles per hour.

The Beaufort Scale is beloved of bar stool experts recounting their experiences. As you learn to match the prevailing conditions with the Beaufort Force, you will begin to suspect that old Jim, whose midship section is the pride of the local brewery, is actually rather unlikely to have been skimming his son's Laser across the wavetops in a Force 8 last Sunday fortnight.

The information you need from your Marinecall service is the expected windspeed and direction in your local waters at the time you expect to be launching *and for the next few hours.*

Consider the wind in relation to the tide. When both are in the same direction the waves will not be too big but when the tide turns and the wind is against the tide, a nasty chop can develop.

Consider the wind in relation to the shoreline. If it is blowing on to the shore there might be quite a surf running and launching will be difficult. If it is blowing off the shore *beware!* The shoreline will appear deceptively calm and it is only after going afloat that you will realise the full strength of the wind. Remember you will have to beat back to the shore in a wind which becomes progressively more gusty as it is influenced by any surrounding buildings.

Consider any forecasted change in wind direction. You may wish to change your itinerary if the passage home is likely to be uncomfortable.

In unsettled weather, don't venture too far from the shore. Learn to recognise the dark line which heralds the approach of a weather front. Keep a look-out for large black clouds which may be bringing a squall with winds up to gale force. Smaller black clouds also bring an increase in the wind. This is a down-draught of cold air and will alter the direction of the prevailing wind, even if only slightly, for as long as it lasts. And never sail in fog.

The downdraught of cold air under a black cloud alters the direction of the wind slightly while it passes

Sea breezes

On a hot, summer day the land heats up and in turn heats the air immediately above it. The hot air rises and cooler air from the sea moves in to replace it. Thus the sea breeze is set in motion.

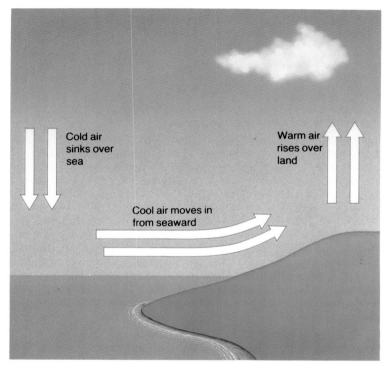

Cold air
sinks over
sea

Warm air
rises over
land

Cool air moves in
from seaward

How a sea breeze is set in motion

Later in the day, as the land cools faster than the sea, the whole process is reversed and a land breeze is created.

The direction of the sea breeze is predictable for any given sailing area. If the day's prevailing wind is from the same direction the sea breeze will fill in smoothly and reinforce it — sometimes until the afternoon brings very strong winds indeed.

If the prevailing wind is from a very different direction, there will be a period of calm while the sea breeze fights to establish itself. This may last only a few minutes before the wind fills in from a completely different direction. Or it can last for the rest of the afternoon, the prevailing wind returning only as the land starts to cool again.

GETTING AFLOAT

It's possible to ride a horse without ever having to catch one and put its bridle on. It's possible to learn to ski without ever understanding how the boots stay clipped to the skis. And there are people who go sailing without ever learning how to rig and launch a boat. But they cannot claim to be sailors and will probably never do more than pull a few ropes at the command of others. It's a recipe for boredom, even seasickness.

The first rule is to take the boat close to the water before pulling up the sails. Take care, though, not to be a road-hog. Be considerate to others and make all possible preparations well out of the way so that you will be at the water's edge for the minimum time possible.

Then make sure that you know where the wind is coming from. Flags and other boats' sails are a good indication.

With the sails and control ropes all ready, move the boat into its launching position and make sure that the front is pointing directly into the wind before attempting to pull up the sails. If you do this, the sails will just flap like flags straight down the centre line of the boat. If the wind is coming over the side of the boat there is a danger that the sails will fill with wind and pull the boat over, damaging it, others and other people. You will not be popular. If the wind is coming over the back of the boat the effect will be even more dramatic. Please don't try it.

A boat is a delicate piece of sports equipment and can be damaged if handled carelessly. The builder has made the boat as light as possible for the best possible performance. The designer has ensured that she is strong enough to carry her full crew when her hull is supported by water. NEVER climb into a boat on dry land. You may go straight through the bottom.

If at all possible, the boat should not be allowed to sit on a beach and should certainly not be dragged into the water on her own bottom.

The boat should have a launching trolley which fits properly. The trolley should carry the weight of the boat on her strongest point — along the keel — and chocks should support her bottom panels where they are strongest as they take the turn into the side panels.

The jigsaw puzzle

The rig

Most modern dinghies have triangular sails. It doesn't take much imagination to accept that each of the three corners needs to be controlled if the sail is to do its job.

The front, bottom corner is fixed. So is the top corner, but it is so high off the ground that it has to be pulled into place with a rope. The back, bottom corner is free to move and so alter the angle of the sails to the wind.

With one of the richest of all sporting languages, it soon becomes impossible to progress with a sailing manual without using a few technical terms. We'll keep them to a minimum.

A singlehanded dinghy has only one sail. On a boat with two sails the larger sail is called the **mainsail**. The smaller sail in front of, or **forward** of, the **mast** is called the **jib**.

1. Hull
2. Mainsail
3. Jib
4. Mast
5. Gaff (not present in most modern dinghies)
6. Boom
7. Rudder
8. Daggerboard
9. Sail battens
10. Kicking strap

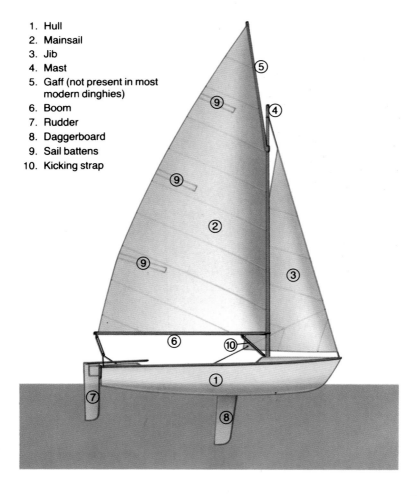

The jigsaw puzzle – 1

The front edge of the jib is stretched taut between anchor points at the front of the boat and on the mast. Special hooks called jib hanks keep this one close to the forestay

Hoisting the mainsail. The rope which hoists a sail is called a halyard. It is led from the top of the sail, up and over the top of the mast and down to a fixing point at the bottom of the mast

The front edge of both sails is held taut. The mainsail is attached to the mast and the jib is usually attached to the **forestay**, one of the three wire **stays** which hold the mast upright. The other two are called **shrouds**.

The rope which is used to hoist a sail is called a **halyard** and each sail has its own.

Very often the sail of a singlehanded dinghy has a pocket, or **sleeve**, which fits over the mast so a halyard is not needed.

The bottom edge of the mainsail is attached to the **boom.**

Battens may be used to maintain the correct aerofoil shape in the back of the mainsail.

To alter the angle of the sail to the wind more rope is needed. A rope which does this job is called a **sheet**.

The sheet for the mainsail is led round **blocks** to provide a two-, three- or even four-part purchase to help the helmsman pull the sail in.

A rope or wire strap called a **kicking strap** is rigged between the boom and the bottom of the mast to stop the boom lifting too far.

A lot of new words. So far, a rather uninteresting chapter. Perhaps the pictures will help.

The sail is pulled in and out according to the direction of the wind by a rope called a sheet. This is the simple mainsheet system of a Mirror

Many dinghies have mainsheet systems in the middle of the boat. This one is on an Optimist

13

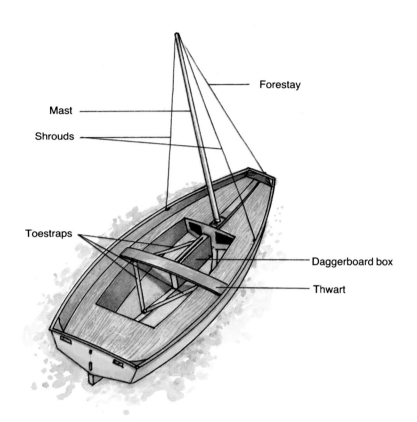

Mast

Shrouds

Forestay

Toestraps

Daggerboard box

Thwart

The jigsaw puzzle – 2

The hull

Only a few new words here, for the moment, starting not with the boat at all but with the people in it. The person who is driving is the **helmsman**, a word which refers correctly to man or woman. NOT, please, "helm". The helm is the steering apparatus itself, not the person using it. Everybody else in the boat is the **crew**, even if there is only one person.

The crew (and here we include the helmsman, too) sit in the **cockpit**, just like the crew of an aeroplane. The cockpit is the open area of the boat.

Close-up of a Mirror rudder and its fittings. Notice the small clip above the lower fitting. This prevents the rudder floating up and off its fittings

The boat is steered by a **rudder**, which hangs on the back on special fittings. A **tiller** is attached to the top of the rudder to bring control of the steering to the helmsman's hand. Most dinghies have a **tiller extension** fitted to the front end of the tiller to allow the helmsman to move his weight around the boat while he is steering.

Only one more item to worry about at the moment: the **daggerboard**, a wooden plate which can be moved up and down in the **daggerboard box** just like a dagger in its sheath.

The kicking strap is rigged between mast and boom to control the height of the boom. Notice how the daggerboard fouls the kicking strap when it is raised

15

A word of warning about daggerboards: when in the fully raised position they will not allow the boom to swing across the boat. So don't put the daggerboard in its box until the boat is afloat. It's a good idea to paint a line across it at its "safe height". It is possible to sail with the daggerboard in the half-way position on all points of sailing, so in the early stages do not raise it so high that there is a risk of it jamming against the boom.

Older designs and larger boats like the Wayfarer use a **centreboard** instead of a daggerboard. The difference is that a centreboard is housed permanently in a longer box and pivots on a bolt. It does the same job — and that is to stop the boat sliding sideways across the water. More of that later.

Buoyancy

To ensure that they neither sink nor fill with water after a capsize, dinghies carry reserve buoyancy, even if their hulls are built of a floatable material such as wood.

This buoyancy is commonly to be found in the form of air tanks, built in to the construction. Blocks of foam may be incorporated to keep the boat floating high in the event of structural damage. The tanks usually have hatches, or at least drain holes, so that they can be dried out ashore. These are a potential source of leaks when the boat is inverted and should be checked regularly. Hatch covers and bungs must always be in place before a boat is launched.

The Mirror has its reserve buoyancy in the form of built-in tanks. The air in these tanks keeps the boat floating high when she is capsized. The red webbing straps are toestraps

Inflatable buoyancy bags are another option. It is easy to see whether they are still doing their job: a deflated bag spells potential trouble. What may not be obvious is how well they are fixed in the boat. They have to keep a heavy weight afloat so the strain on their fixings is enormous. Webbing straps, passed through the locating loops, must be fastened securely in the boat and the locating loops on the bags must never themselves be relied on to hold the bag in the boat.

The cockpit of the 8 ft Optimist children's dinghy, showing securely fixed inflatable buoyancy bags

Where to sit

Crews will be disappointed to read that the helmsman's comfort is most important. He must be well braced and have the best possible vision. The responsibility of balancing the boat rests with the crew and if that means crawling into an uncomfortable corner sometimes . . . well, so be it. In practice, a compromise can usually be reached.

The helmsman's ideal position is on the **windward** side of the boat; that is, the side from which the wind is blowing. The sail will be set on the opposite side, **to leeward** (pronounced "loo-ard"), its weight balancing the weight of the helmsman and not obstructing his vision. He will hold the tiller in his back hand and the mainsheet (the sheet which controls the mainsail) in his front hand. He will change hands when he changes sides.

Where to sit in a gentle breeze. The helmsman is holding the end of the tiller extension in the back hand. The mainsheet is led across the body and held in the front hand. The helmsman is sitting on the windward side of the boat and has a good view ahead

Webbing straps are usually fitted in a dinghy and held a few inches above the floor with a length of shockcord. These are **toestraps**. Helmsman and crew can use them when sitting on the side deck to anchor their feet positively in touch with the boat.

On those occasions when he needs a third hand, the helmsman can lay the mainsheet across the top of the tiller and trap it with his thumb.

When the helmsman needs a spare hand, he can trap the mainsheet against the tiller extension using his thumb. The thin rope glued round this tiller extension is to provide a good grip and prevent it from slipping through the fingers when wet

Ready . . .

It may seem strange, but advice on how to set off from the shore does not appear until a later chapter. We recommend very strongly, and therefore assume, that there is an experienced assistant on hand for the first few outings to make sure that the boat is prepared correctly, that the weather conditions are safe and that you set off in the right direction.

If your adviser does not think of it, check that each sheet has a figure-of-eight knot tied at the very end of it, to prevent it disappearing through the system and out of reach. Remember that there are two jib sheets.

The mainsheet should have an extra knot tied in it at a position which prevents the boom from being let out too far. In a boat with shrouds, the extra knot should prevent the boom crashing into the leeward shroud if the mainsheet is let out quickly. In a singlehander, the extra knot should prevent the boom from setting square across the boat — worse, forward of square! More of this in Thursday's section.

Transits *If two objects which are apparently in line in front of you remain in line, you are travelling straight. If the further object apparently moves to one side of the nearer object, your boat is being swept off course in that direction*

Steady. . .

By now you should know exactly where the wind is coming from. Sail to an unobstructed area of water and "park" the boat while you find your sea legs. Orientation at sea is not as easy as on land and you will soon learn to use transits to help you to steer a straight course. Moored boats (provided you don't hit them), chimneys, prominent buildings, harbour walls (not too close please) and maybe navigation buoys (don't obstruct commercial traffic) are all suitable. Moving targets are not.

Stop

The sails are used to drive a boat. It is logical, then, that if they are not used the boat will stop. A good temporary "parking" position is known as **lying-to** and it involves positioning the boat so that the wind is blowing across the side. The sheets are allowed to run free so that the sails are streaming away from the helmsman, across the other side of the boat like flags.

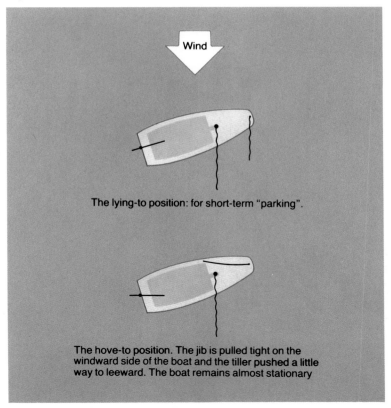

The lying-to position: for short-term "parking".

The hove-to position. The jib is pulled tight on the windward side of the boat and the tiller pushed a little way to leeward. The boat remains almost stationary

Lying-to. 'Look Mum, no hands!'

The daggerboard/centreboard should be about half-way down.

There are two ways of slowing a boat which is sailing. One is to push the tiller away so that the front of the boat turns into the wind. The other is to let go the sheets so that wind is spilled from the sails. A combination of the two should be used until the boat is lying-to.

The front of the boat should not be pointed directly into the wind in order to stop. This brings the boom over the heads of the passengers, which makes life uncomfortable. It also reduces the manoeuvrability of the boat and starting her moving again will prove difficult.

Accelerating

In the lying-to position the helmsman will be sitting on the windward side of the boat with the wind blowing on to his back. The crew of a two-man boat will probably be sitting in the middle, facing forward.

Both should check the surrounding water for obstructions and other boats before moving off. The helmsman should make sure that the wind is blowing across the side of the boat and should look for a suitable object some distance ahead, to give him something to aim for while he familiarises himself with the feel of the steering.

The tiller should be held centrally to keep the boat pointing in the right direction while the mainsheet is pulled in steadily until the mainsail starts to fill with wind. At this stage the boat will start to move forward.

The crew should be ready to move his weight to join the helmsman on the windward side of the boat, if needed. As the sails fill with wind the boat will tend to lean over and it is crew weight which must keep her upright.

As the breeze increases the crew weight is moved further to windward to keep the boat level. In his normal sailing position the helmsman will stay further outboard than the crew so that he can see where he is going

In practice, the crew will probably stay in the middle of the boat for the first few outings in light winds.

When the helmsman is comfortable and in control of the boat, the crew can pull in the jibsheet to fill the jib with wind. The same comments apply. More crew weight may be needed on the windward side. Make all sail adjustments gradually.

Steering

From the start, try to regard the tiller and tiller extension as one piece of equipment. The helmsman will be infinitely more comfortable, and therefore more efficient, sitting on the side deck holding the end of the tiller extension than he will if he is crouched in the confines of the cockpit holding the tiller awkwardly.

Oh dear, NO! The helmsman is holding the tiller, not the extension, and therefore is sitting inboard and leaning forward in an effort to see round the crew. And look out for the boom hitting that raised elbow!

All alterations of course should be made smoothly. Jerky movements of the rudder will shake the sails and upset the boat's performance.

Unless a big change of course is being made, rudder movements should be only small. If the tiller is a very few degrees away from central the boat will change direction.

Sitting in his correct position, the helmsman pushes the tiller away from him to turn the front of the boat towards the wind and pulls the tiller towards him to turn the front of the boat away from the wind.

In simple terms: tiller moves right, front of boat moves left; tiller moves left, front of boat moves right.

Try small, gentle movements of the tiller for as long as possible before making the first turn.

Turning round

It's time to go back the way you came. Look behind and choose a suitable transit, somewhere in the area of your starting point.

Make sure that the sheets controlling the sails are not knotted up and will run out freely if necessary. You will be turning the boat so that the front passes through the wind. Check that you will not be turning into an obstruction or an approaching boat.

A boat which has stopped will not turn. Keep the boat moving forward steadily. Make sure the crew is ready and push the tiller away hard. WAIT. Cross the boat as the front passes through the wind and the boom swings across. Don't forget to duck!

For the first few times, you can let the sheets go as the boat makes the turn. That should make it easier to change hands on the tiller as you change sides.

As soon as the boom is safely on the other side, look up, centre the tiller and identify your chosen transit. Check that the wind is, indeed, coming across the side of the boat and that you really are heading back the way you came, pull the sails in and off you go.

Pulling in the sails

It is not true that the harder the sails are pulled in, the faster the boat will sail. A sail must be set at the correct angle to the wind to drive the boat at her fastest.

It's easy to work out where the sail should be. Pull in a flapping sail until it stops flapping. As simple as that. The difficult part is to avoid pulling it in too far. An experienced helmsman is making constant adjustments to keep the sails set perfectly.

A singlehander has only one sail to worry about. He should pull it in until it just stops flapping and hold it in that position for his chosen course.

The principle is the same in a two-sail boat. First the angle of the mainsail should be established, then the jib. At this stage the jib can be held in position by a **cleat** and the helmsman can use the front edge of the jib to tell him if the wind changes, or if he is wandering away from his course. When the front of the sail starts to flap, the front of the boat is pointing too close to the wind.

Stopping

No harm in repeating the message about stopping. In a popular sailing area, until you know the right-of-way rules, it may be necessary often.

Push the tiller away from you a little — not too much — and let the sails go completely. The boat will turn closer to the wind and all the driving force will be spilled from the sails. If in doubt, turn towards the wind to avoid a collision. If you turn away from the wind you will probably accelerate. If you have misjudged the situation it is better to make contact while slowing down, rather than at high speed.

The jib sheet is led through an eye fitting called a fairlead and can be held in place by a cleat. This type has moving jaws which clamp onto the rope

SAILING CLOSE TO THE WIND

Points of sailing

There are three main points of sailing, which describe the boat's progress in relation to the wind direction. When the wind is blowing across the side of the boat, as it was yesterday, the boat is sailing **on a reach** or **reaching**.

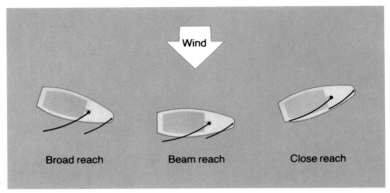

Reaching

Yesterday's point of sailing was a **beam reach**, with the wind blowing square across the side of the boat. If the wind is blowing from further forward, the boat is sailing on a **close reach** (she is sailing closer to the wind). If the wind is blowing from over the back corner, the boat is sailing on a **broad reach**.

If the wind is blowing from behind the boat, she is **on a run** or **running**. The other point of sailing, and today's goal, is the **beat**.

A boat is **on a beat** or **beating** when she is sailing as close as possible to the direction from which the wind is blowing. We can shorten that mouthful by calling it simply **to windward**.

No boat can sail straight into the wind. As a rough guide most will sail at an angle of 45 degrees to the wind so a journey to windward will have to be made in a series of zig-zags. This is known as beating. Each part of this journey to windward is called **a tack** and when the boat changes course on to a new tack she is **tacking**.

And that's just what you did yesterday. Every time you pushed the tiller away, and you and the sails changed sides, you were tacking the boat.

Beating is no more complicated than yesterday's exercise of reaching, tacking, and sailing back on a reach again — but concentration is needed if it is to be done well.

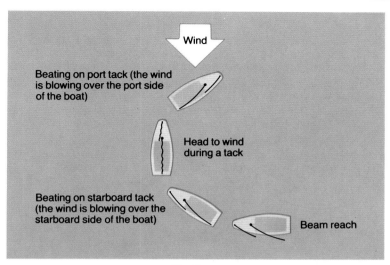

Wind

Beating on port tack (the wind is blowing over the port side of the boat)

Head to wind during a tack

Beating on starboard tack (the wind is blowing over the starboard side of the boat)

Beam reach

Beating

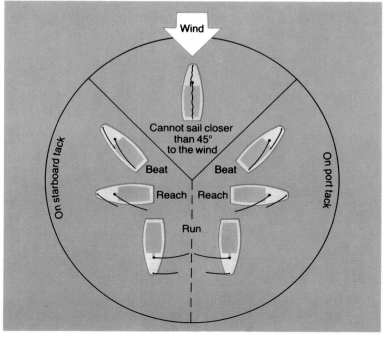

Wind

On starboard tack

Cannot sail closer than 45° to the wind

Beat   Beat

Reach   Reach

Run

On port tack

Points of sailing

Reefing

In some boats it is possible to **reef**, that is, to reduce the area of the sail when sailing in strong winds. There are many different methods but the most common involve taking a large tuck along the bottom of the mainsail.

If your dinghy's sail is easy to reef, don't be afraid to use the facility. The simplest form of reefing is to tie short lengths of line through special **reefing eyes** in the lower part of the sail and around the boom, using a reef knot. Individual lengths of line can be replaced by a single lashing.

Singlehanders with sleeved-luff sails can be reefed by rolling the sail round the mast to reduce sail area. The Topper is particularly good at this and the manoeuvre can even be carried out at sea successfully.

The sail of a Topper can be reefed simply by rolling it round the mast. Because the sail has no sail battens, any number of turns can be taken round the mast until only a pocket handkerchief is left!

Beating

So . . . check the wind direction and settle down in the lying-to position again. Pull the sails in and steer the boat until she is sailing on a reach at about 90 degrees to the wind. So far, so good, that's what you've been practising.

Lower the daggerboard to the fully-down position.

Now push the tiller away from you gently but firmly — but not far enough to make the boat tack. When the front of the boat is pointing a little closer to the wind, bring the tiller smartly back to the centre of the boat and keep her sailing in that direction.

Notice that the boat has slowed down and that the sails are beginning to flap. And notice *where* the sails are beginning to flap. It is at the front, vertical edge: the **luff**. Watching the luff of the sails is a vital clue in sailing the boat well, especially to windward. When the luff begins to flutter, power is being lost. The remedy is to pull the sail in tighter, until the fluttering stops.

When the front edge of the sail flaps, the sheet should be pulled in to bring the sail and boom closer to the centreline of the boat

At this point, unless the wind is very light, something else happens. Something which can be unnerving if it is unexpected. The boat leans over. The sheer weight of wind in the sails pushes the boat out of vertical. The bigger the sails, the more the boat leans — or **heels** to use the correct term. It is not, by the way, "listing". That's what happens to ocean liners which are about to sink.

When the sails are pulled in hard on a beat, the boat starts to heel

The closer a boat sails to the wind, the more she tends to heel. That is one reason why early experience should be on a reach in a light wind.

A keelboat has her heavy keel to counterbalance this heeling tendency. The weight in her keel will allow her to heel only so far and no further.

A dinghy is a different kettle of fish. The only extra weight in a dinghy comes in the form of helmsman and crew. They must use their weight to counterbalance the dinghy's heeling. If they do not, she will continue to heel until she capsizes.

So what should they do? Easy. Sit on the windward side of the boat. The wind is pushing her over **to leeward**, so the crew weight is needed **to windward** to bring her upright again. Every effort should be made to sail a dinghy upright. Keelboats are designed to sail well at an angle of heel. Dinghies are not. The most forgiving designs, like the little Mirror, will simply not give of their best. There are, however, some dinghies which become quite difficult to sail if they are allowed to heel too far.

Moving crew weight further to windward counteracts this

Now try that again. Push the tiller away until the boat points closer to the wind. Then pull in the sails until they stop fluttering. Adjust crew weight to keep the boat upright. Sail on until you are happy with the feel of the boat.

Repeat the exercise, allowing time between each adjustment to settle down, until you believe that the sails are pulled in as tightly as possible. At this stage the boat should be sailing as close as possible to the wind. Now for the acid test.

Tack the boat. Take it gently. Let out the sheets a little and concentrate on bringing the tiller back to the central position fairly quickly after the front of the boat has passed through the wind. Position yourself on the new windward side of the boat, feel for the wind on the back of your neck and set off on a reach again, just like yesterday. Now gradually push the tiller away to bring the boat closer to the wind, pull in the sails and assume a beating course on the new tack.

That's all there is to it. All you need now is practice. And more practice. And more. Sailing a boat well to windward is not just a matter of personal pride and, perhaps, of winning or losing an important race. In extreme circumstances your boat and your life could depend on it.

On inland waters where, no matter what happens, you will eventually wash up against a bank, this may seem to be an over-dramatic statement. Caught at sea, unable to make any progress to windward against a tidal stream, you would not be the first small boat sailor to be towed home by the life-boat. But what happens when the life-boat isn't there?

With practice, there will come a time when you will know how close the boat will sail to the wind and will be able to position her instinctively, pulling in the sails at the same time to assume a beating course. Soon, you will be able to tack quickly from a beat to a beat, rather than lose time (and distance) by starting off on a reach again, with the sails flapping.

Knit one, purl one

Of course, it won't go right every time. Once you start using the cleats to hold the sails in place you may leave one cleated accidentally during a tack. At worst, the result will be an undignified capsize. Turn to Saturday's chapter.

A more common problem is that the helmsman stops the boat in mid-tack by bringing the tiller back to the centre too quickly. The boat is just sitting there, sails flapping, boom swishing back and forth over the helmsman as he crouches in the bottom of the boat, hardly daring to lift his head to ask where his boat is going. The answer, embarrassingly, is "backwards". She's not sailing anywhere. She is being pushed along by the wind. And as she is pointing directly into the wind, she can't be going forward.

At this point, technical sailing manuals will explain how the rudder works in reverse when the boat is sailing backwards. But we hadn't planned to cover that until Saturday's chapter. So this is what to do for the time being.

Grab the jib sheet close to the sail and pull it right out to the side of the boat. Never mind which side. Hold on to it until the sail starts to fill with wind, apparently from the wrong side, and the boat starts to turn. When you judge that she has turned so far that the wind is now blowing across the side of the boat, let go the jib sheet, sort yourselves out and start again. Don't try to use the tiller during this manoeuvre. It may do more harm than good. Just hold it firmly in the centre of the boat.

Filling the jib on the wrong side of the boat like this is called **backing the jib** and it is a technique which is often used to assist boats such as catamarans which are slow to tack.

A backed jib. In this example the boat is 'hove-to', a more permanent position than just 'lying-to'. With the jib backed and cleated in position and the mainsail completely free, the boat won't move much

If the boat has only one sail, there is no jib sheet, so grab the boom and push hard. Push the tiller away in the same direction. Remember, PUSH. PUSH. The boat will turn to leave you sitting on the windward side, ready to have another try.

Analysing the tack

So far, circumstances have said "tack!" and you've muddled through somehow. There must have been occasions when you have lost the end of the mainsheet, dropped the tiller, become disorientated or felt as though a giant squid has somehow wrapped itself around your feet.

Most of this can be avoided by adopting a logical tacking sequence which co-ordinates hands and feet. The one described below is a good starting point but there is no reason why you should not make a few subtle changes to suit your own sailing style as the months progress.

Aft mainsheet

Aft simply means towards the back of the boat. So this method will work with any dinghy which is rigged in a similar way to the Mirror and the Topper.

Both tiller and mainsheet are aft of (behind) the helmsman so it makes sense to face aft during a tack. Most dinghies are small enough to require little more than a shift of body weight to move from one side of the boat to the other.

Feet

Consider the feet first, then, and remember the three Fs . . . **front foot forward**.

Adopt a comfortable sailing position on the side deck with the feet free to pivot and move. Kick the heap of unwanted mainsheet towards the back of the boat, out of the way. Allow the back foot to support the body comfortably vertically below the knee and extend the front foot towards the centreline of the boat, but not too far. It must be able to take your weight as soon as you stand up.

Allow the back foot to support the body comfortably vertically below the knee and extend the front foot towards the centreline of the boat

Go into a standing crouch with the weight on the front foot, pivot on that foot and approach the new side deck bottom first. Keep your head down!

During the tack, go into a standing crouch with the weight on the front foot, pivot on that foot and approach the new side deck bottom first. Keep the head lowered, well out of the way of the boom as it crosses the boat.

Tacking: both crew members slide across the boat in unison, keeping her upright throughout the maneouvre

If you are the sort of dancer who needs to watch your feet to make sure that they are still on the end of your legs, you could try this exercise at home, using two dining room chairs to represent the side decks. If another member of the family can be persuaded to hold a tiller and a mainsheet for you, these homework sessions can become quite sophisticated.

Hands

While sailing, it is the back hand which holds the tiller, the front hand which holds the mainsheet. If you have already developed an infallible method of tacking by using the back hand to push the tiller away then by all means stick with it.

If changing hands during the tack is still something of a hit and miss exercise, try this.

Change hands before tacking. Using the thumb of the back hand to hold the mainsheet against the tiller extension (see Tuesday), take the end of the tiller in the front hand. Take the mainsheet in the back hand and check that the mainsheet is quite separate from the tiller.

Using the front hand, push the tiller away to start the tack. You should soon find that the foot-swivelling, bottom-wiggling progress across the boat blends smoothly with the movement of the hands which automatically finish the manoeuvre in the correct position for sailing off on the new tack.

Centre mainsheet

Lasers, Optimists and many two-man racing dinghies favour a mainsheet system in the centre of the boat. While sailing, there is little danger of the sheet becoming entangled with the tiller but during a tack the scope for confusion is endless.

If the boat has a cleat for the mainsheet, the first job is to uncleat it and check that it is free to run in an emergency. Then kick the unwanted sheet forward, out of the way.

Feet

If the mainsheet is forward of you, you should face forward when tacking. **Forward** is the opposite of aft: it means towards the front of the boat.

Everything we said about foot positioning in the section on aft mainsheets holds good for boats with centre mainsheets **except that** it is the **back foot** which leads across the boat.

Hands

There is no need to change hands before the tack and there should be no need to separate the mainsheet and tiller! Just push the tiller away, using the back hand and keep hold of the mainsheet with the front hand during the tack.

The next part sounds complicated but is surprisingly easy in practice. Provided you don't drop anything vital during the manoeuvre you will find yourself sitting on the new side deck with the tiller in your front hand, held behind your back, and the mainsheet in your back hand, held across the front of your body.

From this strange position only two small arm movements are needed to return to normal.

Move the back arm backwards and outwards, letting a little mainsheet slide through the hand if necessary, until it reaches the tiller. Grab the tiller and keep steering a straight course, thumb clamping the mainsheet to the tiller. Let go the tiller from the front hand, which is then free to take the mainsheet and cleat it if required.

Traditional commands

Whether, at a later stage, it amuses you to test your crew's reflexes by tacking without warning or whether you adopt a verbal shorthand such as "now" or "let's go!", you should know the commands which most of us learn as beginners.

The helmsman who wants to tack says clearly to the crew "ready about!". The crew replies briefly, loudly and succinctly. As the helmsman pushes the tiller away from him he calls "lee-oh!"

Traditionalists and big-boat helmsmen sometimes use the phrase "helm's a lee". It means quite literally that the tiller is already on the leeward side of the boat and things are starting to happen . . . fast.

The crew's duty

At the call of "ready about!" a good crew will quickly check the water ahead and to windward for any obstructions or approaching boats which the helmsman may not have seen. At the same time, he uncleats the jib sheet but holds it tightly so that the sail does not lose its efficiency. It is possible that the helmsman will change his mind and he won't want the boat to slow down unnecessarily.

It is only after the call of "lee-oh!", when he is sure that the boat has started her turn, that the crew frees the jib sheet, making sure that it will not snag as the jib changes sides. He crosses the boat, taking the new jib sheet with him and cleating it without delay as the boat settles on the new tack.

If the crew finds that the kicking strap is in his way during a tack, he can face aft.

SAILING DOWNWIND

The run

At this stage you may be forgiven for asking why we have left what is apparently the easiest point of sailing until the end. But we haven't.

With the wind blowing from behind, the image of a boat skimming along gracefully, like a feather on a lake, is a hard one to shake. Sometimes it is true. In light weather, there's not a lot to upset the apple cart. In stronger winds, in gusty winds and in waves, though, care is needed.

Probably the main reason for leaving the run until last is that changing direction introduces a new manoeuvre: the **gybe**, during which it is the back of the boat which passes through the wind.

A few more nautical terms

Telling you to turn the front of the boat towards the wind is using plain English but it doesn't always make for easy reading. Now that you have grasped the concept of which way the boat is supposed to be going in relation to the wind, try these few words.

The front of the boat (as if you didn't know really) is called the **bow** — sometimes even the **bows**. The back of the boat is the **stern**. The flat vertical panel right at the back is called the **transom**, a word we introduce simply because the rudder is hung on the transom. Old salts may talk of a "stern hung rudder" but it isn't strictly accurate to talk of the rudder being hung *on* the stern.

We return to the word **luff**. We have already met it when it means the front edge of a sail. Now we meet it as a verb. **To luff up** means to turn the bow of the boat towards the wind — to push the tiller away from you, if you are sitting in the approved position.

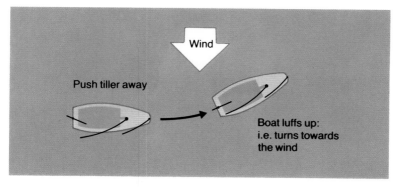

Wind

Push tiller away

Boat luffs up:
i.e. turns towards
the wind

The opposite manoeuvre is **to bear away** — to pull the tiller towards you in order to turn the bow of the boat away from the wind.

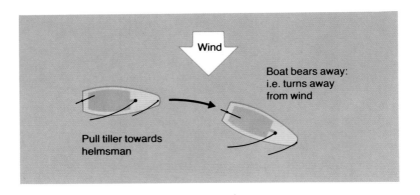

Wind

Boat bears away:
i.e. turns away
from wind

Pull tiller towards
helmsman

Finding the wind

The wind will have taught you many lessons by now, not least that it is never perfectly steady. Inland sailors will have learned this rather more quickly than sea sailors, because of the way in which trees and buildings conspire to blanket and funnel the prevailing wind.

Even at sea the wind is always on the move, oscillating up to 15 degrees on either side of its mean direction on a day when it appears to be steady.

Identifying these little vagaries of the wind when running before it is a skilled task and one best left to the racing helmsman who is in training for a place in a world championship team. The rest of us can just sit back and enjoy the ride, without having to work hard to prevent the boat heeling over. Or can we?

Just sit back and enjoy the run? Not always! You should stay sharp!

That's better! The helmsman is sitting to windward and the crew must therefore be to leeward to keep the boat level

Let's set off on a reach again, the wind blowing across the side of the boat, the daggerboard half way down. To alter course so that the front of the boat turns away from the wind, we must pull the tiller towards us (**bear away**). But not too far.

At the same time the sheets must be let out smoothly so that the sails are set *almost* horizontally across the boat.

Remember that word *almost*. The knot that you tied in the mainsheet (see Tuesday) to prevent the boom lying square across the boat will come into its own now. If you positioned the knot accurately all you need to do is let the mainsheet run until the knot reaches the take-off block.

To find out whether you are on the right course you can again watch for flutter along the edge of the sail. But this time the back edge is more important than the front edge.

If you have turned so far away from the wind that it is now blowing from the other side of the mainsail the back edge will start to flutter and you should immediately push the tiller away from you to bring the front of the boat closer to the wind.

If the wind catches the mainsail from the wrong side when the boat is running it may gather enough strength to push the sail unexpectedly through almost 180 degrees to land with a thump on the other side. To the occupants of the boat it will come as an unwelcome surprise, especially if somebody's head meets the boom as it swings across.

If the sail is let out to its running position and the front edge is fluttering it is telling you, as it was before, that the wind is blowing from too far forward of the boat. You can either pull the sail in until the fluttering stops or pull the tiller towards you until the whole sail is full of wind.

As you are practising sailing on a run, choose the second option and steer to the wind.

In a two-sail boat the jib can offer an extra clue to the wind direction. If it can be made to fill with wind on the same side as the mainsail you are doing well. If it flops about and even tries to set on the other side, it is being blanketed from the wind by the mainsail. This means that at any moment the wind may catch the mainsail from the wrong side and flip it across the boat. Push the tiller away to bring the front of the boat a few degrees closer to the wind.

If the jib is pulled in too tightly on a run, it will 'backwind' the mainsail and power will be lost

There is a temptation to sheet the jib in too hard on a run, because it looks better. Try to resist this. It will only stall and reduce the pulling power of the mainsail by "backwinding" it.

Crew weight

With the sail let right out for the run, there is very little tendency for the boat to heel so the weight of the crew will not usually be needed up on the windward side deck.

The singlehanded helmsman will have to slide inboard a little to keep the boat upright.

The helmsman of a two-man boat is better off. He can stay up on the side deck if that is the position he prefers and ask his crew to move over to leeward to balance him. He should be warned, however, that most good crews do not take kindly to being dunked under water by a helmsman who allows the boat to heel unnecessarily.

The gybe

Changing course from one reach to another, or from one tack to another, involves turning the front of the boat through the wind (tacking).

To alter course by tacking when sailing downwind is wasteful of sea-room and can actually be difficult to achieve successfully and safely. The boat is on a course which is up to 180 degrees away from the wind. By the time she has turned that far, and is pointing directly into the wind in the middle of her tack, she has lost all her momentum and becomes difficult to manoeuvre.

So all we do is to turn the other end of the boat through the wind. It is already pointing the right way and the alteration of course is only a small one.

Turning this way is called **gybing**.

The most important difference between tacking and gybing is which end of the boat passes through the wind.

The secondary difference, but the most important consideration to the crew, is that during a tack the boom travels only a short distance and cannot build up a great deal of speed on its journey. During a gybe, the boom is travelling from side to side of the boat and can come across at high speed. Don't forget to duck!

Commands

To make quite sure that both members of the crew know which way the boat will be turned, the commands for a gybe should differ from those for a tack. "Stand by to gybe" and "gybe-oh!" are recommended.

The gybing manoeuvre

Back to the dining room chairs again.

With an aft mainsheet system, the helmsman will still face aft. With a centre mainsheet system, the helmsman will still face forward. It's the soft shoe shuffle as before.

It is in the handling of the tiller that the gybe differs from the tack.

Sorting out the knitting before the gybe. Make sure the mainsheet is not entangled with tiller or feet. Swivel the tiller extension to leeward, ready for immediate use after the gybe

To initiate the gybe, the tiller is pulled towards the helmsman, to turn the front of the boat a little further away from the wind. This brings the wind to the "wrong" side of the mainsail — something we were trying to avoid when simply sailing on a run.

If you are still finding it comfortable to hold the end of the tiller extension while sailing on a run, it is a good idea to swing it across to the other side of the boat before initiating the gybe.

You may, however, have decided to sit further inboard and fold the tiller extension back along the tiller, using the tiller itself to steer downwind. Even if you are steering with the tiller extension, you might like to try folding it back along the tiller during the gybe, to tuck it neatly out of the way.

Whatever your choice, you will be holding the end of the tiller itself, not the extension, as you pull it towards you to go into the gybe.

Tiller, boom and helmsman should all be on the centreline of the boat at the midpoint of the gybe

Helmsman (and crew if there is one) should cross the boat at the same time as the boom. The helmsman should bring the tiller back to the centre line as soon as the boom swings across.

Tiller, boom and helmsman should all be in the middle of the boat at the same time during a gybe.

If there is more than one crew member, distribute their weight evenly about the boat and tell them to sit still and duck their heads, leaving the helmsman to balance the boat.

Handling the mainsheet

To provide a buffer, the mainsheet should be pulled in a little just before the gybe. With practice, the helmsman will be able to time the arrival of the boom on the new side with letting out the mainsheet to act as a shock absorber.

Changing hands

It is both possible and advisable to change hands on tiller and mainsheet before the gybe with both aft and centre mainsheet systems. There is plenty of scope for something to go wrong and if the helmsman is in position he is better equipped to counter it quickly.

Complications

The most common unwelcome sequel to the gybe is the **broach**. The mainsail slams across too quickly, fills with wind too quickly and turns the front of the boat towards the wind too quickly for comfort. The boat heels over, the boom end may dig in to the water and a capsize is often the result in strong winds.

The antidote is simple but must be administered without delay. The boat must be brought upright and the helmsman must pull the tiller towards him smartly to make the boat turn away from the wind. (This assumes that he has reached his new position on the new windward side of the boat and is not lying in the bilges with his braces caught round the mainsheet block.)

The crew of a two-man boat must pull the jib in quickly on its new side. That will help to turn the front of the boat away from the wind.

The most common sequel to a bad gybe is the broach

ATTENTION TO DETAIL

It's time to think not just about sailing, but about sailing well.

Whenever you come across a similar boat going your way, sail along behind for a while, watch what the crew is doing, how the sails are set and compare a well-sailed boat with your own. Copy what the experts are doing and see whether you can stay in touch or whether they start to open the gap between you.

This is where a sailing school environment is so good. Once you have mastered all the different points of sailing you will be able to test your skills against your fellow students around a short race course. Nothing serious yet, just sailing in company in order to identify strengths and weaknesses. Some schools will show a video of your efforts later in the day to reinforce what you already suspected!

Even if you are in a minority of one, the time has come to set targets. Choose three or four markers — buoys, moored boats — and set yourself a triangular or rectangular course. Make sure that one of the legs is directly into the wind. Sail round the course a few times, timing each lap. If one lap takes much longer than all the others, ask yourself why.

Balance

Sailing a dinghy upright is not just a matter of looking good. You will have found out by now that trying to keep a comfortable seat in a boat which is heeled over a long way is difficult. The last thing you want when the boat is out of balance is for the helmsman or crew to fall over.

Don't be afraid to hang right out over the side to prevent the boat from heeling

A boat which is heeled over too far is either spilling wind from the sails or actually having her sails pinned down by the wind. Both are undesirable.

Something which does happen as the boat heels is that she starts to turn into the wind. The helmsman will find that the steering has become very heavy.

Steering

If the tiller is off-centre, so is the rudder. A few words, then, about how a boat's steering works.

When the boat is moving, water is flowing past the hull; past the rudder, too. If the rudder is in a straight line with the hull the water flow is uninterrupted. If the rudder is to one side or the other the flow of the water is deflected and this is what causes the boat to turn.

Taking the extreme case, if the rudder is turned at right angles to the hull the boat will stall because it offers too much resistance to the water trying to flow past it. To the water, it is like hitting a brick wall. The brake is on. The boat becomes unmanageable.

Even if the rudder is turned through only a few degrees, it is still acting like a brake. So for optimum performance, try to use it as little as possible.

Trim

Trim is just another word for balance fore and aft. There is no mystique attached to it. The boat designer has gone to a lot of trouble to work out the best possible underwater shape for his boat. Look at the boat as she floats in the water, upright, before you step aboard. Your ambition should be to keep the same area of boat under the water while you are sailing.

Correct trim

Weight too far forward: the bow is hitting each wavelet like a brick wall

When the crew weight is too far back, the transom and rudder dig into the water and create turbulence which slows the boat and can affect the steering

With the designed number of crew on board, a dinghy will almost certainly be trimmed well enough if everyone is sitting fairly close together, comfortably, on the seating or decking provided, towards the middle of the boat. As confidence grows, it is sometimes a good idea to shift the crew weight slightly forward when the boat is on a beat, to give the slimmer "nose" more chance to bite into the waves.

In strong winds, reaching and running, crew weight should be moved back to stop the front of the boat ploughing into the waves.

Daggerboard

Only an expert worries about the precise position of the daggerboard. Recreational sailors do not need to lose any sleep over the question.

The daggerboard is an essential piece of the boat's equipment because it helps to prevent the boat sliding sideways over the water. This can be demonstrated easily by holding a knife blade in a jug of water. In one direction the blade can be moved easily through the water. In the other, it offers considerable resistance.

It is when a boat is sailing on a beat that she most wants to slide away to leeward. By lowering the daggerboard fully, the boat is prevented from doing so and she will take the line of least resistance by travelling forward.

On a beat, then, the daggerboard should be in the fully lowered position.

On a run there is very little sideways force in the sails so little or no daggerboard is needed. However, a fully raised daggerboard can be awkward — it is in the way when gybing, for instance, and it obstructs crew movement. There is also a tendency for the boat to become skittish without a small amount of daggerboard protruding through the slot. The ideal position for the board on a run is about three-quarters raised, provided the crew remembers to lower it into a safe position before a gybe.

In between, there is the reach. On a beam reach, which is where we started this book, the daggerboard should be in the half-way position, being raised progressively as the boat sails on a broader and broader reach, that is, nearer to a run. A close reach requires the daggerboard to be almost fully lowered.

In practice, a boat can be sailed on all points of sailing with the daggerboard half down, although her progress to windward will not be efficient. There are only three "don'ts".

Don't sail with the board fully down on a run if there is any weight in the wind: a sudden wild gyration can sometimes cause the boat to "trip over" the daggerboard.

Don't try to sail close to the wind without a daggerboard. You may not move forwards at all but you will certainly slide sideways.

Don't try to bear away from a beat with the daggerboard fully down. It may prove to be very difficult and can put unnecessary strain on the boat's gear.

When the conditions are good — warm water, sunshine and a light breeze — try these "don'ts" for yourself. Learn to identify the feeling of having no daggerboard and of having too much.

Tides

For those sailing on tidal waters, knowing the time of high water is almost as important as checking the weather forecast.

Tide tables, available at boat shops, tourist information offices and many seaside gift shops, tell you more than whether or not there will be any water to sail on.

The height of the tide is usually given alongside the time. It is important to the big-boat sailor, of course, because he wants to know the depth of water under his keel. But it is of interest to the dinghy sailor, too.

For one thing, it gives an indication of how fast the tidal stream will be. The very high tides, **spring tides**, are fast flowing because a lot of water is on the move between one high water and the next. High water mark is much lower at **neap tides**, which do not have such a strong flow. Spring tides come in a long way and go out a long way. The difference between high and low water mark on neap tides is considerably less.

The state of the tide must dictate launching tactics in many places. It may not be possible to launch and recover a heavy dinghy which needs a vehicle and winched trailer in certain places at certain states of the tide. On a simpler note, it's always a good idea to leave the launching trolley where you are sure it will be high and dry on your return.

Off a simple coastline, the tidal stream will flow one way on the flood (the incoming tide), the opposite way on the ebb. Locals will let you know how fast. The flow accelerates towards half tide and then slows again. At the turn of the tide there will be a brief period of slack water.

The tidal stream inshore, in shallow water, will tend to be slower than it is further offshore, in deeper water.

The flow will be stronger in deep water channels, so it pays to know where these are.

Mooring buoys, moored boats and posts provide evidence of the tidal flow, if needed. Just sail close enough and you will be able to see which way the water is moving.

Sailing in tidal waters

Apart from the obvious consideration of not being left high and dry when the tide goes out, it makes sense while learning to avoid sailing if the tidal stream could carry you into danger. For example, if the wind and tidal stream are in the same direction and there is no landfall downwind and downtide for many miles, it is foolhardy to set sail on a broad reach or run. If the wind is very light or very strong it is foolhardy to set sail at all.

In tidal waters you will not be the only person needing sea-room. Commercial craft will be making their way into nearby ports and harbours. If you have ever heard that power should give way to sail this is a good time to forget it. Large powered vessels have absolute right of way when manoeuvring in restricted waters. It is up to you to find out where the main shipping channels are and avoid them.

There will be times when allowance must be made for the tidal stream when sailing from one point to another. If you are planning a passage of several miles, say along the coast to the next town, it will pay handsomely to make sure that the tidal stream is going your way. If the wind is light and your best speed through the water is 3 mph and you are sailing into an adverse tidal stream of 2 mph, your speed over the land will be only 1 mph. A journey of three miles will take three hours. If that tidal stream were in your favour, the same journey would take considerably less than an hour.

But you don't have to be going a long way before the question of tides crops up. Just a short hop from the shore to a point a few hundred yards away still calls for a little thought.

Say you are setting off on a reach from the slipway to visit a friend on his moored cruiser. The wind is blowing across the left hand (**port**) side of the boat. The tidal stream is moving from left to right. If you aim directly at the cruiser on a beam reach the tide will set you down so that you will end your trip having to sail on a beat.

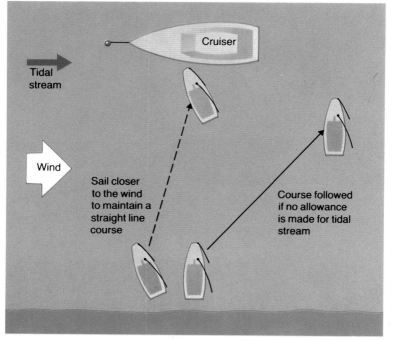

Allowing for the tidal stream

In this example you should start on a close reach, aiming at a point to windward of where you want to finish, so that your course sailed is a straight line, not a curve.

You can check your progress at any stage by "taking a back bearing". That is, look over your shoulder as well as ahead to keep your boat on a straight line between your launch point and your destination.

Sailing in light winds against a tidal stream can create the illusion of progress when in fact you are moving backwards. Choose transits on the shore to check your progress and consider anchoring to avoid being swept too far down on the tide.

Planing

There are two main types of boat hull, **displacement** and **planing**. A displacement boat is sturdily built and pushes her way through the water like a big ship. A planing hull, given enough power, will lift up and skim across the top of the water. Racing powerboats and ski boats are good examples.

Given enough wind, a dinghy will lift and skim, or plane, across the wavetops. These are Enterprises

Planing: sails set to perfection, plenty of wind and crew weight a little further back than usual to keep the bows lifted clear of the waves

Modern dinghies will lift on to a plane, too, in the right wind conditions.

There has to be rather more wind than you need when learning — perhaps 15mph or more. The boat has to be on a reach because she will not generate enough speed when beating. Sails, daggerboard, balance and trim have to be as near perfect as possible and the boat will start to lift on her "shoulders" (the area around the mast where the narrow front merges into the wider back sections) and plane across the water.

This is one occasion when crew weight really is critical. The crew members should move aft of their usual beating position, but not so much that the back of the boat is digging in to the water. If this happens the boat will have great difficulty in lifting on to the plane or, as powerboat drivers sometimes call it, "getting over the hump".

If she carries a large sail area, or if the wind is very strong, a dinghy will plane on a run. Some extreme designs are also said to plane to windward but as a rule they gain extra speed by bearing away a few degrees.

Surfing

Even if there is not quite enough wind to promote planing, a boat can be encouraged to surf down the waves. Sorry, inland sailors, this happens only at sea.

The waves have to be coming up behind the boat and as the behaviour of the waves is closely linked with the direction of the wind, this means that the boat must be on a reach or run before she has the opportunity to surf.

As the wave lifts the back of the boat she will start to accelerate. The luff of the sail will start to flutter because her sudden increase in speed creates an "apparent wind" from further forward than the real wind. It is the same as the cooling breeze which is so welcome to the cyclist free-wheeling down a hill.

Pulling in the sail sharply as the luff starts to flutter helps the boat to catch the wave and surf along it. With practice, it is possible to "pump" the sail several times on each wave like a bird's wing to extend the surfing time. But don't do it in a race. It is not allowed.

Knots

At last, an opportunity to do something useful with all those bends and hitches you learned in the Scouts or Guides.

You do not need an armoury of knots to be able to survive afloat. Learn them as you need them and remember that the most important characteristic of any nautical knot is that it will not let go until you want it to . . . and then it must be capable of being untied easily after it has been under tension and soaked with water. You can survive for a long time with just a figure-of-eight knot and a round turn and two half-hitches. Learn these first.

Be careful where you tie knots. Apart from the stopper knot at the end, never tie a knot in any rope, such as halyards, sheets or control lines, which may need to be let out in a hurry.

A **Reef Knot** has earned the reputation of being the sailor's most important knot. In fact, it has few uses outside reefing the sail. It is a neat, flat knot but it can easily capsize and turn into two loose half-hitches.

Reef knot

A **Clove Hitch** is useful for securing a rope to a post quickly.

Clove hitch

A **Round Turn and Two Half-hitches** can be used for the same purpose.

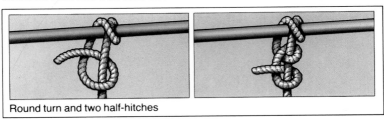

Round turn and two half-hitches

A **Bowline** is a wonderful knot and can be used to form a loop or to tie anything to anything, where a looped attachment is acceptable. Its disadvantage is that it cannot be untied under load.

Bowline

A **Figure of Eight** knot should be tied without fail in the end of every halyard, sheet and control line on board, to prevent them passing back through their various sheaves, blocks and cleats.

Figure of eight knot

A **Rolling Hitch** is said by some to be more difficult to learn than all the rest put together. It is useful to know, however, in some towing situations. The tow boat streams a line astern and each boat is secured to it, one behind the other, with a rolling hitch.

Rolling hitch

Using a horn cleat

A cleat — any cleat — is no more than a temporary means of keeping a rope in place. The rope must be capable of being let go in a big hurry. Therefore resist the temptation to take a locking turn around a horn cleat. Wind the rope round in a figure of eight a couple of times and let friction take care of it. That way it can always be undone quickly.

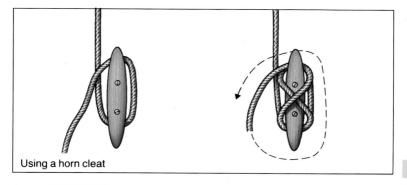

Using a horn cleat

Coiling

Halyard tails, painters, tow-ropes and anchor lines are usually coiled to keep them tidy. Match the size of the coil to the length and diameter of the rope to be coiled — bigger loops for longer, fatter ropes. Keep the coil sizes even. Avoid twists in the rope. Don't tie a knot in the end: the coil may be needed in a hurry.

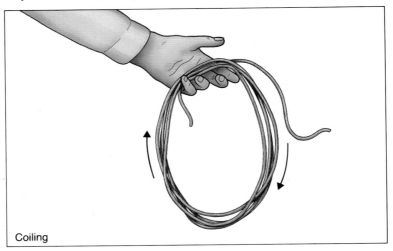

Coiling

Anchoring

The majority of dinghy sailors will not need to use an anchor. However, if you carry an anchor you should know how to use it. Here, as briefly as possible, are the basics.

The larger and heavier the anchor, the better it will hold the boat in position. Without going to ridiculous extremes, this should be borne in mind when choosing the right anchor for the boat. Dinghy anchors are usually lighter than the ideal because of the constraints on space and weight. The local chandler will advise.

Lightweight dinghies do not carry anchor chain but rely instead on a lightweight line, called an **anchor warp**, whose breaking strain must be greater than the weight of the boat and her crew. The length of this line should ideally be five times the depth of the water in which the boat will be anchored.

If you do decide to anchor frequently, you would be well advised to add two or three metres of chain between the anchor and anchor warp. If it is to hold a boat securely, an anchor must dig in to the seabed at a shallow angle. The chain helps to hold it close to the horizontal. A vertical pull releases the anchor.

A boat does not park neatly above her anchor. She will drift downwind, or downtide (whichever is the stronger), until she reaches the end of the scope of her anchor warp.

If there is no special anchoring post in the boat, the inboard end of the warp can be tied securely round the bottom of the mast. The boat will ride to her anchor most comfortably if the warp is led over the bow. If there is no special fitting for this, a short length of line can be used to make a loop to hold the warp close to the forestay.

Before throwing the anchor over the side, check these few points:–

1   Is there plenty of room for the boat to swing round the anchor — even to drift downwind/downtide if the anchor drags?
2   Is the anchor warp secured to the anchor?
3   Is the other end secured to a strong point in the boat?
4   Is the warp coiled neatly and is it ready to run out freely?
5   Is anybody standing in or on the coils of the warp?
6   Are there any underwater obstructions? (Underwater cables are marked by large notices onshore.)
7   Are you on the edge of a channel?
8   How deep is the water and have you enough warp?
9   Which way is the tidal stream?

If wind and tide are going the same way, you should approach the chosen anchoring spot under full sail, turn the boat head to wind, that is, with the front pointing directly into the wind, and drop the anchor. When you are happy that the anchor is holding securely, raise the centreboard and drop the sails.

If the wind is against the tidal stream, you should sail a short distance upwind of your chosen anchoring position, drop the mainsail and sail to the chosen spot under jib, before dropping anchor.

BASIC SEAMANSHIP
Launching

Wind along the shore

This is the easiest possible launch.

Take the boat close to the water, turn her head to wind, pull the sails up, tension them for the conditions, check that everything is secure, that there are knots in the end of the sheets, that the sheets themselves are free to run, that the self-bailer is not in the down position, that the bungs are all in tightly. Put the rudder on and fix the rudder blade in the up position.

Wheel the boat on its trolley, stern first, into the water. Pull the trolley out as soon as the boat floats and let somebody take it up the beach for you, while you hold the bow of the boat into the wind.

As soon as the crew is ready, help him into the boat and ask him to sit in the middle, being prepared to pull in the leeward (seaward) jib sheet and balance your weight as you climb aboard.

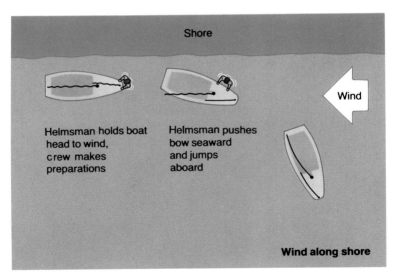

Launching

In one smooth, effortless move, push the bow of the boat seaward and spring lightly aboard as the crew pulls in the jib and lowers the daggerboard to half way. Lower the rudder blade, take hold of the mainsheet and sail to deeper water for a final gear-check.

Wind offshore

This time you can ask the crew to hold the bow of the boat while you go aboard to prepare for take-off. When you are in position, tell him which way to push the bow off as he jumps aboard. With a good strong push in flat water you may be able to sail off with the rudder blade slightly lowered and a few tweaks of the mainsheet. Otherwise the crew can **back the jib** (see Wednesday) as he comes aboard.

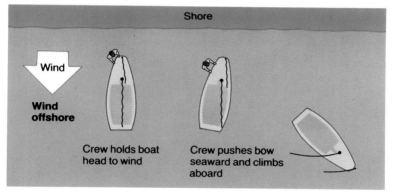

Shore

Wind

Wind offshore

Crew holds boat head to wind

Crew pushes bow seaward and climbs aboard

Wind onshore

This can be tricky if there are waves breaking on the beach. Somebody has to get very wet while the bow is being held. The boat must be launched bow-first and extra care must be taken that she does not bounce on the trolley or the beach in the breaking waves.

On an exposed shore, conditions may call for a co-ordinated effort from a competent crew using full sail in order to drive the boat through the surf. A few clubs have a support boat available to pull dinghies off the shore, others use ropes so that crews can pull themselves into deeper water. The majority don't. Remember, if you don't have the experience to cope with difficult launching conditions, you don't have the experience to come ashore safely either.

On inland waters it may be possible to leave the sails down and row or paddle into deep water before hoisting . . . but not in strong winds . . . and not in confined waters.

Returning to shore

Wind along the shore

Returning to the shore on a reach poses no problems. The daggerboard can be removed completely a few yards from the shore, provided the helmsman has allowed for the boat to drift sideways after that happens. The sails can be let out little by little to slow the boat on her final approach and, when she reaches shallow water, the helmsman can luff head to wind while the crew jumps overboard to hold the bow.

Wind offshore

A more tedious approach. The boat will be beating into a gusty wind with calm patches and must keep her daggerboard lowered for as long as possible. It is just a question of patience, of sailing as well as possible until the daggerboard is in danger of touching the bottom, then raising it and sailing on until the crew can jump over into relatively shallow water.

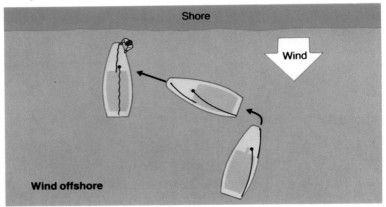

Shore

Wind

Wind offshore

Wind onshore

Time for some seamanship. Even if others are racing up the beach under full sail, don't be tempted to follow suit. Choose an area of clear water as close to the beach as sensible, turn head to wind and lower the mainsail. Sail in under jib.

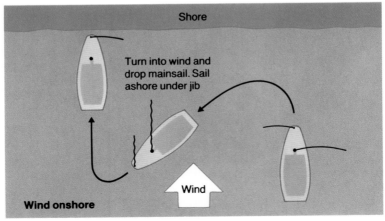

Shore

Turn into wind and drop mainsail. Sail ashore under jib

Wind

Wind onshore

Returning to shore

Disregard this advice if sailing from a beach with big breaking waves.
Sometimes a full-scale assault on the beach at high speed under full sail is
essential if the boat is to land clear of the breakers. Take local advice and
never allow the boat to turn side-on to the waves when beaching.

*A seamanlike approach to the land when the wind is
blowing onshore*

The crew as an anchor

It is no use expecting the crew to be in control of the boat if he is standing
in chest-deep water. As soon as the water is above his waist his body
buoyancy starts to lift his feet off the bottom and reduces his usefulness as
a mooring post.

That's the good news for crews. The bad news is that in deep water,
sending the crew over the side to hang on to the bow of the boat is a
recognised method of keeping the boat head to wind!

Capsize

The dreaded word! But why should it be? A well-prepared dinghy won't
sink and the worst damage is likely to be to the crew's ego.

There might be something to be said for starting every sail training course
with the boat on its side in the water and the crew swimming.
Unfortunately, few sailing schools enjoy the warm water and sunshine
which make this a viable proposition.

Instead, an early opportunity must be taken to try out the capsize drill at the end of a session, with the promise of a hot shower.

The earlier you make a successful recovery from a capsize, the quicker you will gain confidence. Try it on Day 1 if you have an experienced assistant.

The most difficult part of capsize drill is actually tipping the boat into the water in the first place. Self-preservation takes over and somebody jumps for the high side! But we'll assume that the boat is on her side and the crew members have both fallen into the water on the cockpit side.

Both crew members are wearing good buoyancy aids (aren't they?) so they will float comfortably without having to put their weight on any part of the boat. This is important. Weight in the wrong place now might turn the boat completely upside-down which in itself is not a disaster but in shallow water can lead to damage to the mast.

This is not to say that the crew should let go of everything and allow the boat to drift away. The golden rule when in any sort of difficulty at sea is **stay with the boat**.

When both crew members have found each other and disentangled themselves from the rigging, the helmsman should swim to the back of the boat to free the mainsheet and check that the rudder is still in place. He holds on to the knot at the end of the mainsheet (so that he stays in contact with the boat) and swims along what ought to be the underwater side of the boat until he reaches the daggerboard.

The crew makes his way back along the cockpit side of the boat and checks that both jib sheets are free. If the daggerboard is not fully lowered, he should push it gently into the lowered position — but not before he has shouted a warning to that effect to the helmsman! All communication between helmsman and crew during these manoeuvres can be made through the daggerboard box itself rather than allowing a shout to die on the wind.

The crew's final task is to find the top jib sheet and throw it over the top of the boat to the helmsman. Warn him about this, too. The helmsman, in return, should confirm that he has caught it.

Only at this stage should the helmsman let go of the mainsheet.

The crew now lies in the water opposite his normal sailing position, allowing his buoyancy aid to keep him afloat. He need not, and should not, hang on to the boat while the helmsman pulls her upright.

The helmsman braces his feet against the hull and pulls hard on the jib sheet and, lo and behold, the boat comes upright. As it does the crew simply rolls into the cockpit and is ready to give the helmsman a helping hand as he climbs aboard.

Well, it's happened, now what?

Helmsman swims round the back of the boat, holding the mainsheet . . .

. . . until he reaches the daggerboard

The crew throws him the upper jib sheet

Helmsman starts to pull. Crew lies in the water very close to the other side, but does not put any weight on the boat

Sometimes the helmsman needs a little extra weight on the daggerboard!

The crew is scooped in as the boat comes upright

The crew is then in a good position to free any ropes which are tangled and help the helmsman back aboard if necessary

Complications

If the boat is reluctant to be righted, the helmsman can climb on to the daggerboard. A belly-flop is usually sufficient. In extreme cases it may be necessary to stand on the daggerboard and continue pulling on the jib sheet. Check that the crew has passed the correct jib sheet over the boat. Trying to pull the boat upright using the lower one is doomed to failure because you will be trying to pull up a jib full of water as well.

If the boat turns into the fully inverted position, don't panic. Climb on to the upturned hull and pull the daggerboard into the fully lowered position. Stand on one side of the hull, with the wind at your back, and pull on the bottom (skyward!) edge of the daggerboard until the boat is lying on her side. Then pick up the righting procedure from the appropriate point.

The dry capsize

If you're quick it is quite possible to capsize and recover a dinghy without even getting your feet wet.

Helmsmen of singlehanders become particularly adept at this manoeuvre and it has become a recognised way of "parking".

The 'dry' capsize

As the helmsman feels his boat reach the point of no return, he scrambles nimbly over the high side and on to the daggerboard. When the time comes to sail off again, he uses just enough weight on the daggerboard to start the recovery and scrambles just as nimbly back into the cockpit as the boat comes upright.

It is at this point that he realises there is no such thing as a dry capsize. The sail shakes itself like a dog after a swim and its entire soggy burden runs down the back of his neck.

Sailing without a rudder

Rudderless sailing sounds daunting but is something which can be learned from only a very few words. Only practice will bring perfection — and it is a skill which is worth cultivating against the day when the rudder might break or the water might be so shallow that it is necessary to sail some distance with it in the raised position.

First you must understand how the sails balance the boat.

Sailing without a rudder – at first there will be much flapping of sails as the crew adjusts to the behaviour of the boat. With practice, it should appear from a distance that the rudder is still in use

It is the jib which pulls the front of the boat away from the wind. The mainsail turns the boat into the wind. Pull in the jib sheet and the front of the boat will start to turn away from the wind. Now pull in the mainsheet until the boat turns back to the required course. From now on it's trial and error and teamwork.

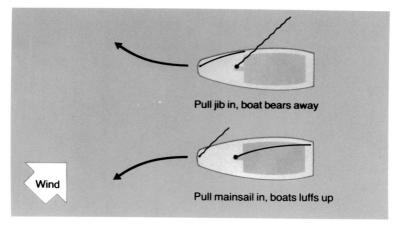

Pull jib in, boat bears away

Wind

Pull mainsail in, boats luffs up

Sailing without a rudder

Heeling the boat assists the steering. We have already mentioned that the boat tends to luff up when she heels over to leeward and this can be used to help her to tack without a rudder.

Heeling the boat to windward will make the boat bear away and can be used to reinforce the power of the jib.

During all these manoeuvres the daggerboard should be raised to approximately half way.

Sailing backwards

If you sail where launching is cramped you might find this one useful. If not, you may never need it.

To set off, the boat must be head to wind. Keeping the daggerboard in the half-way position and the tiller central, push the boom out as far as it will go. You will find yourself on a run, but going backwards.

At this point life becomes a little tricky. The rudder works in reverse. If you push it to the right, the front of the boat (the *real* front) will turn to the right. Don't over-steer. Because the rudder is now effectively at the front of the boat, the steering is very susceptible to small alterations of rudder angle.

Man overboard!

A rather sinister heading for an exercise which may never be needed in anger. It is a useful boat-handling experience, though, and may well be used if an item of boat gear is dropped over the side.

Let us assume that the helmsman has fallen overboard. The crew's first job is to regain control of the boat by freeing all the sheets and putting the boat into the lying-to position.

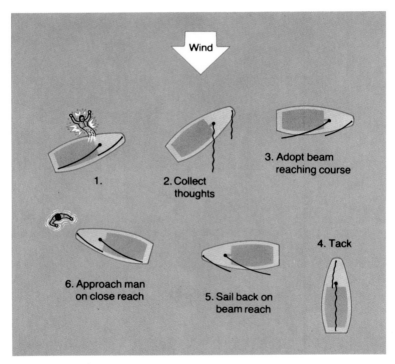

Man overboard!

He should then sheet in gently and start the boat sailing on a beam reach. As soon as he is ready, he tacks the boat and sails back on a beam reach. This should bring him on approximately the right course to come alongside the helmsman in the water.

He should make the final approach on a close reach and stop the boat, just to leeward of the helmsman, by letting out the sails. He should pull the tiller up to windward after the boat has stopped to prevent the boat turning into the wind as the helmsman comes aboard over the side.

Ever decreasing circles

Probably the best boat-handling test of all is to sail the boat in a small circle. Start off by sailing around a moored boat, paying attention to the position of the daggerboard, crew weight distribution and set of the sails so that at any given instant everything is in its correct place. Gradually tighten the circle until you are sailing under perfect control within a couple of boat lengths of the chosen obstacle.

Now stop worrying the owner of that moored boat and find yourselves a patch of clear water. Try again, aiming for smaller and smaller circles until it becomes impossible to keep re-positioning the daggerboard. Raise the daggerboard half way and see if you can spin the boat in her own length.

Rules of the road

1   Power gives way to sail. But don't count on it.

A deep-draught boat manoeuvring under power in a navigation channel has right of way over a shallow-draught sailing boat. Therefore a sailing cruiser with her engine turned on may have right of way over a dinghy under sail.

A minority of speedboat and water scooter drivers do not know the right of way rules. You may be unlucky enough to meet one.

2   A sailing boat on starboard tack — that is, with the wind blowing over the starboard side of the boat — has right of way over a sailing boat on port tack. This holds true for every point of sailing from the beat to the run.

3   An overtaking boat must keep clear of the boat she is overtaking.

4   When two boats are on a converging course, the boat on the windward side must keep clear.

5   In a narrow channel, drive on the right. When crossing a navigation channel, take extra care and cross at right angles in order to clear the channel as soon as possible.

Those are the main points. If you have right of way, **hold your course**. If you alter course just as the other boat is altering course to miss you, a serious accident could occur. If you think the helmsman of the other boat is unaware of the approaching collision, **shout**. If he still fails to take avoiding action, it is up to you. Failing to avoid a collision puts you in the wrong, regardless of who had right of way in the first place.

Emergency equipment

A boat which is well-built, well-maintained and checked regularly for signs of wear and tear does not need to be overburdened with spare parts while she is sailing. There are a few items which should be carried, though, if only for peace of mind.

A paddle is essential. The wind often dies in the evening and it can save a long drift home. If you contrive to lose it overboard, there are substitutes:

the spinnaker pole serves surprisingly well. In the hands of a strong crew a daggerboard makes a wonderful paddle.

A bucket is a must for boats which take in a lot of water during a capsize. If the water level is above the daggerboard slot opening it must be bucketed out very quickly indeed. Boats which come up nearly dry from a capsize might actually find a large bucket to be a nuisance. A small plastic bailer or sawn-off polythene bottle of the right size and shape is a good alternative.

An anchor is recommended. With good judgement, you will never have to be taken off your damaged boat and leave it anchored, to be salvaged later. But these things do happen. A light dinghy anchor with a rope of a length appropriate to your sailing waters will save you having to find a spare mooring buoy if you want to stop for lunch. Or you may find it impossible to sail against the tidal stream. You could anchor and wait for help.

Life-boat crews like small boat sailors to carry a waterproof pack of mini-flares. Letting off the flares at, say, ten-minute intervals gives you a very good chance of being picked up quickly. It takes about five minutes to scramble the life-boat after your distress signal has been seen and reported, so they could be afloat just in time to see your second one.

Whatever you decide to carry, it will be no good to you if it floats away when it is needed most. Before going afloat each time check that every item of loose equipment is tied in to the boat.

A **painter**, that is, a sturdy length of rope attached to the bow, is not really an item of emergency equipment because it will probably be used every time you launch and recover the boat. It is included here because it leads us neatly to think about being towed.

Towing

Usually, the club's motor-boat which arrives to tow your boat home will throw you a line, but it is better to use your own painter when towed by anyone else. Most boat owners are pleased to help someone who is in difficulties but there are laws governing claims for salvage and a tiny minority of "helpers" are actually quite mercenary!

If there is a special mooring or towing fitting on the foredeck of your boat, so much the better. If not, take the towing line round the mast and tie a reliable knot, such as a bowline or a round turn and two half-hitches. Lower the sails, raise the daggerboard to at least half way, move the crew weight aft and steer a course to follow the towing vessel.

MORE ADVANCED SAILING

Matching the sail to the weather

Without delving into aerodynamic theories, it is enough to say that a full sail will develop more power than a flat sail.

All we need to worry about at this level is that if the wind is blowing hard, all the control lines should be pulled out as hard as possible, provided that this does not create unsightly creases across the sail.

Apart from making sure that the halyard is as tight as humanly possible, there is little to be done to the jib on most simple dinghies. One way to ensure that the luff of the jib is really taut is for one person to pull forwards as hard as possible on the boat's forestay while another tensions the halyard on its cleat. This pulls the top of the mast forward and shortens the distance between the top and bottom corners of the jib luff, so that when the forestay is let go the jib luff comes under tension.

'Swigging' the halyard: pull outwards to achieve greater tension and hold that tension while making the rope fast

If the jib is attached to the forestay by jib hanks, tension is achieved in a similar way, but by "swigging" on the halyard. Hoist the jib first.

Swigging

'Scolloping', resulting from a slack jib halyard

It follows that the main halyard, too, must be taut.

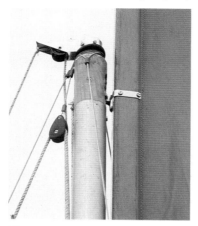

The halyard fitting on the gaff of a Mirror should fit snugly into the hole in the top of the mast

If it doesn't the result is . . .

. . . a sail which has these horrible creases

*Even when the boat is sailing hard, the creases which result
from a slack halyard are not flattened out by the wind. You
won't win any races like this*

The shape of the mainsail is adjusted by the controls at the two bottom
corners, the **downhaul** and the **outhaul**. The downhaul, naturally enough,
adjusts the tension in the luff and the outhaul adjusts the tension along the
foot of the sail. Used together, these controls can flatten a sail
progressively for the prevailing conditions.

*A simple downhaul system on a Mirror. The control line runs
from the front of the boom, up and through an eye in the
sail, down and round a block on the other side of the boom
and back to a cleat within easy reach of the crew*

A similar system is used to adjust the outer end of the mainsail foot – the outhaul

For strong winds, the mainsail foot can be stretched tightly along the boom to take some of the fullness out of the sail. Most of the creases will be blown out when the boat is sailing – but even if they are not, these are not detrimental to the boat's heavy wind performance

If the bottom, front corner of the mainsail (the **tack**) is pinned in place, there will be an eye made into the sail a few inches above it. A line led through this eye and round the appropriate fittings does the same job as a downhaul, but is called a **Cunningham** control line, after the man who introduced the concept.

Tensioning the downhaul (Cunningham) pulls the fullness, and hence the centre of effort, of the sail forward. We promised not to become technical so we'll simply say that this produces a good aerodynamic shape for sailing on a beat.

Looser foot to put more shape into the sail for medium breezes

On a reach and run, fuller sails are the order of the day so both downhaul and outhaul may be loosened.

In its simplest form, the kicking strap is used to keep the boom more or less horizontal. If the boom is allowed to lift at its outer end the mainsail twists. In light to medium breezes this presents no great problem, except that a lot of wind is spilled from the top of the sail unnecessarily. In heavy weather, this twisting causes the boat to become unbalanced, hence unstable, and the run becomes rather more exciting than it need be.

If the kicking strap is too loose the boom will lift on a run, allowing the sail to twist and 'spill' much of the wind which should be driving the boat forward

Technical racing dinghies use powerful kicking straps to push the boom forward and pre-bend the mast to force a desired shape into the mainsail. Beware of over-tensioning a sophisticated kicker until you understand it fully!

Balance

Having said that a dinghy should always be sailed upright, we now come to the exceptions. A few, and the Topper is one, are designed to sail a little better in some conditions with a small angle of heel. Lifting some of the flat bottom out of the water reduces the wetted area of the hull and reduces drag. Try it when you are sailing well enough to notice the difference.

Most dinghies benefit from being allowed to heel to leeward when beating in light weather, if for no other reason than to persuade the sails to fall naturally into shape under gravity. Reducing the wetted area helps a little, too.

Balance *Singlehanders can be heeled to windward on a run*

Singlehanders can be heeled to windward on a run. With only one sail, they are inherently unstable on that point of sailing and it can help to keep the boat under the centre of effort of the rig. However, this is not a game for the novice. It is all too easy to "step on a banana" and roll in to windward.

The dead run

As soon as you feel confident, you can re-tie the second knot in the mainsheet to allow the boom to be set square across the boat. It will enable you to sail dead downwind, rather than a few degrees higher as you were taught to do in the "training run" position. Watch out for the unintentional gybe, though.

Goosewinging the jib

If you are not using a spinnaker, the jib can be set on the windward side of the boat on a run, to save it being blanketed by the mainsail. You will need a special jib boom, known more commonly as a **jib stick**, or even **whisker pole**. Often, the spinnaker pole itself will do the job. One end of the jib stick is clipped or hooked to a ring on the jib or on to the jib sheet close to the sail; the other end is clipped or hooked on to a special eye on the mast and the sail is sheeted in on the windward side and cleated. Don't be afraid of setting the sails like this: the boat will be better balanced than using the mainsail alone and allowing the jib to flop from one side to the other.

Running goosewinged. The jib is boomed out on the windward side, the opposite side from the mainsail. This is done only on a dead run, when the wind is directly behind the boat

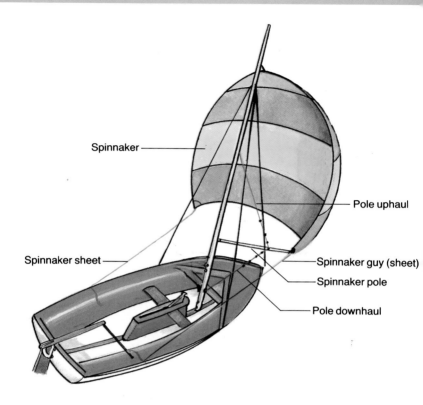

Spinnaker

Pole uphaul

Spinnaker sheet

Spinnaker guy (sheet)

Spinnaker pole

Pole downhaul

Spinnakers

Some boats carry only two sails, mainsail and jib, but many carry a very full sail which balloons out ahead to give them extra speed downwind. This is the **spinnaker**, large, colourful and beloved of chocolate-box manufacturers.

Just a few words to say how a spinnaker is rigged, rather than how you should set about rigging it. If your boat is equipped with spinnaker gear, ask an experienced sailor to sail with you and check it out. If not, sail with an expert and ask his advice on fitting a spinnaker to your boat.

The traditional way to stow a spinnaker is in a bucket tucked neatly in the corner of the cockpit. The spinnaker sheets (or continuous spinnaker sheet) are attached permanently to the two bottom corners but the halyard must be kept out of the way, clipped to the mast, until it is needed.

When the sail is to be hoisted, the end of the halyard is unclipped from its stowage, passed outside the jib sheets and back underneath them to be attached to the top of the spinnaker, still in its bucket.

As the helmsman pulls the sail up, the crew takes the spinnaker pole, clips one end to the windward spinnaker sheet and the other end to the mast. The spinnaker pole is also a boom and needs its own form of kicking strap, called a **pole downhaul**.

The development of the **spinnaker chute** has made spinnaker hoisting and lowering child's play. The sail is stowed in a long sock with the halyard and sheets attached permanently. One end of the halyard is attached to the top of the sail, the other end to a reinforced patch in the centre of the sail. Pull one way and the sail is hoisted, pull the other and it disappears, navel first, into the chute. The pole can be clipped in place before the sail is hoisted.

Setting the spinnaker

Just like any other sail, the spinnaker works because wind is flowing across it. Just like any other sail, if the luff starts to flutter it should be sheeted in, smartly, or it will collapse.

A well-set spinnaker on a Lark. Helmsman and crew are sitting slightly further back than usual to help to promote planing. Notice that the two bottom corners of the spinnaker are level

On a dead run the spinnaker pole is set approximately square across the boat, on the opposite side from the main boom. When using the sail on a reach, the pole is allowed as far forward as possible, until the luff is fluttering so much that it becomes impossible to set the sail.

The height of the spinnaker pole is important. At all times, both bottom corners of the sail should be at the same height.

The jib becomes unimportant when the spinnaker is set. It can be lowered, set as well as possible or, in some dinghies, rolled up on a special furling gear.

The crew must be on his guard all the time the spinnaker is set. The sail is susceptible to the slightest change in wind direction and must be kept pulling, just on the point of fluttering, all the time. It's a good idea to buy the crew a sun visor or special sailing sunglasses. Squinting at the sun through a brightly coloured spinnaker can soon bring on a headache.

Trapezing

Some racing dinghies and catamarans are rigged with **trapeze** wires, attached to each side of the mast, to support the weight of the crew and allow him to stand on the side deck with all his weight outboard.

The extra usable crew weight allows the boat to carry extra sail area, hence it is the faster boats which carry trapezes. Some even carry two, one for the helmsman and one for the crew, but you'll need a few years' experience under your belt before you try one of those.

The crew must put his faith in the helmsman to keep the boat steady and be prepared to move his own weight for small adjustments in balance. In marginal trapezing winds, the movement of the crew as he is perpetually going out on the trapeze and coming in again can slow the boat drastically — to say nothing of the effect on the knee joints of the poor crew! So the helmsman should slide gently in and out if by doing so it is possible to allow the crew to stay out on the trapeze.

An expert crew will trapeze without holding on to the handle and will adjust the hook so that his body is parallel to the water. In the early days, the trapeze ring should be a little higher than those of the experts and the position of the crew can be compared to that adopted when abseiling. When his weight is needed outboard, the crew grabs the handle, hooks his trapeze belt to the trapeze ring and places his forward foot firmly on the **gunwale** (the outer edge of the deck). Using the front leg, he pushes himself outboard and lets go the handle when he is comfortable. At first, the feet should be about two shoulder widths apart on the side of the boat. They should be brought closer together as soon as possible — say, one shoulder width apart — for maximum style and efficiency.

The front leg should be braced at all times, which means bending the back one first. When coming inboard again, lead with the back one.

Under perfect control, the experts make it look so easy. The International Fourteen carries a cloud of sail on a 14 ft hull and allows both helmsman and crew to use trapezes in order to balance the rig. Not one for the novice, this!

Racing

You don't have to enter the national championship. You don't even have to go to the local regatta. But sooner or later it's fun to have a go at racing. And it's a wonderful way to find out how well you are sailing.

The start is the most difficult part. You have to plan to sail across the starting line at exactly the right time. Boats don't stand still, so the race cannot be started like a running race.

A tidy line-up for a start at the national championship of the 14 ft Merlin Rocket class

The starting line can be between two buoys or poles or it may simply be an extension of an imaginary line between two transit poles on the shore.

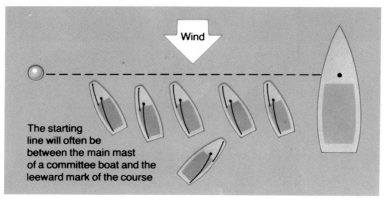

Wind

The starting line will often be between the main mast of a committee boat and the leeward mark of the course

The timing of the start is critical for those who want to win. Each group of boats, usually referred to as a class, is given a ten-minute warning period.

Flags are hoisted and lowered to indicate the passage of time. Each class has its own "warning signal", usually a flag from the International Code of Signals, which is hoisted exactly ten minutes before the start. Code Flag P (the Blue Peter) is hoisted with five minutes to go. Both flags are lowered at the precise moment of start. A hooter or gun draws attention to the flag signals.

Some big fleets use a 'gate start'. A 'pathfinder' boat sails off on port tack, a motor boat follows. Thus a 'gate' is opened between the committee boat and motor boat. The fleet starts in an orderly fashion between the two. This system can save a great deal of pushing and shoving at certain places on the starting line

The course to be sailed will be sketched on a board ashore before the fleet goes afloat. Efforts will usually be made to set the first leg of the course directly to windward because this spreads the fleet efficiently and prevents a log-jam forming as everyone arrives at the first turning mark together.

The Topper's robust construction and simple rig has made it very popular, not only as a beginner's boat but also as a top racing boat. The national championship always attracts a large entry. Notice how some of the lighter and less experienced helmsmen have reefed their sails in these brisk conditions

Club weekend race courses will make use of local buoys. More prestigious events will tend to use a committee boat well away from the shore for starting and finishing. Courses will be more predictable — mostly triangular.

The first leg will be to windward. A red flag (indicating that marks of the course are to be left to port) or a green flag (indicating that marks are to be left to starboard) on the committee boat before the start tells the fleet whether to turn left or right at the windward mark.

There follows a reach to the **wing mark**, a gybe, a reach to the **leeward mark** (which is where we started) before the fleet is away on the windward leg again.

That is the basic triangle. It may be embellished by the addition of a "sausage" in between each triangle, in which case it becomes known as an Olympic course, for obvious reasons. On the sausage stage, the fleet sails directly to the windward mark and back to the leeward mark (in theory, a beat and a dead run), omitting the wing mark.

85

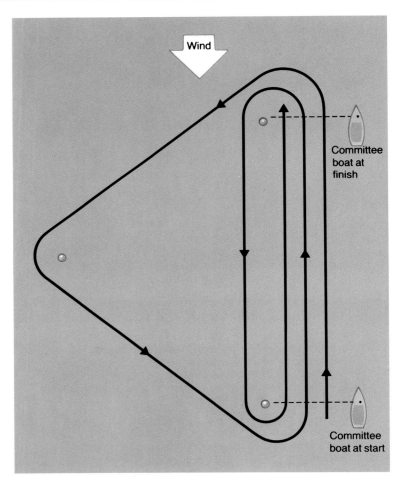

The Olympic-type course: triangle, 'sausage', beat

The committee boat will move to form a finishing line by the windward mark for an important event.

There are many right-of-way rules which govern sailing boats which are racing. There are almost as many publications which explain them. The best way to learn them is by personal experience; pick them up gradually by observing the few basic rules relating to port and starboard, overtaking boat and windward boat situations. Let the others build up by observation, reading the International Yacht Racing Union's Racing Rules booklet and by talking to club experts.

Racing in a big fleet is not for the faint-hearted. In a situation like this it is important to know the racing rules!

GLOSSARY

aft   towards or at the back of the boat

back the jib   pull the jib in hard on the "wrong" side of the boat in order to turn the bow
backwinding   wind blowing into the front of the mainsail from the wrong side, caused by the jib being pulled in too tightly
balance   horizontal levelling of the boat
battens   flexible supports in special pockets to help the back edge of the mainsail to stay in shape
bear away   tiller pulled to windward to turn bow away from wind
beat   course sailed to windward
block   pulley used to increase purchase on a rope tackle
boom   spar which supports lower edge of sail
bow   front of boat
broach   sudden, unscheduled, turn into wind

centreboard   pivoting board in centre of boat to prevent sideways drift
cleat   device to clamp or hold rope in place
Cunningham   system to adjust tension in front edge of sail

daggerboard   board which can be moved vertically in centre of boat to prevent sideways drift
downhaul   rope which controls vertical tension, usually of front edge of sail
downwind   the direction to which the wind is blowing

forestay   wire stay between bow and mast to support mast fore and aft
forward   towards or at the front of the boat

goosewinged   jib boomed out on opposite side from mainsail on a run
gybe   turn so that back of boat passes through wind

halyard   rope used to hoist sail
head to wind   front of boat pointing directly into wind
heel   boat leaning over sideways

in irons   front of boat pointing directly into wind when at sea, boat unable to manoeuvre

jib   front (smaller) sail
jib stick   pole used as boom for jib on a run

keel   central, solid part of hull construction fore and aft; also weighted fin below hull of keelboat
kicking strap   rope or wire strap led between boom and foot of mast to control height of boom

GLOSSARY

leeward   (pronounced "loo-ard") downwind
leeward mark   turning mark at extreme downwind corner of racing course
luff   front edge of sail; to push tiller to leeward to turn front of boat towards the wind
lying-to   boat almost stationary in water, wind blowing across side, sails streaming to leeward

mainsail   principal sail, attached to mast and boom

outhaul   rope or tackle used to adjust mainsail foot tension

painter   rope attached to bow, used to tie up boat
plane   to skim across the top of the water
port   left hand side of a boat, looking forward (colour code: red)

reach   course on which wind blows across side of boat
reef   to decrease sail area
rudder   blade at back of boat, used for steering
run   course with wind blowing from behind boat

sheet   rope which controls position of sail in relation to wind
shrouds   wire stays which support mast sideways
sleeve   pocket in front edge of sail which fits over mast
starboard   right hand side of boat, looking forward (colour code: green)
stern   back of boat

tack   to turn boat by passing front through wind; front bottom corner of sail
tiller   bar attached to rudder to assist steering
transom   flat vertical panel at back of boat
trapeze   wire to enable crew to stand on windward side deck for extra leverage

whisker pole   jib boom (no longer common)
windward   direction from which wind is blowing
windward mark   turning mark at extreme windward end of racing course
wing mark   turning mark between two reaching legs of triangular racing course, also known as **gybe mark**